Facebook Inspiration

30 days of creativity for your page

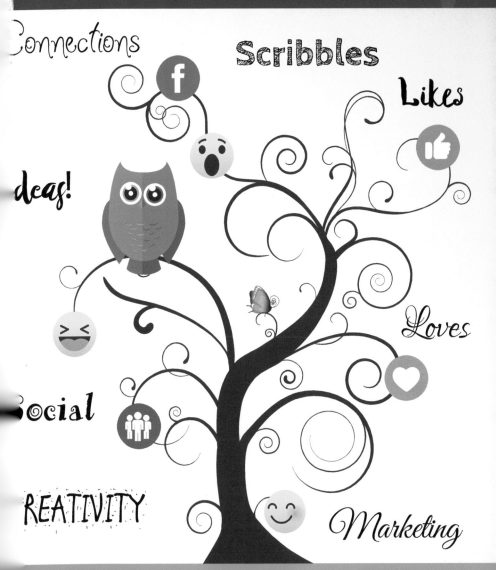

Connections

Scribbles

Likes

Ideas!

Loves

Social

REATIVITY

Marketing

VANESSA HUNT

CONTENTS

DEDICATED TO

My kind, loving Mum, Sally.
Forever in my heart.

ACKNOWLEDGEMENTS

I would like to thank the following people for their support:

To Chrystel Melhuish of Plum Design and Publishing – thank you for your professional advice and creative skills, which have allowed me to achieve my dream of publishing my first book.

To my wonderful husband – thank you for supporting me in everything that I do.

Finally, thank you to all the small business owners and professional friends who were generous with their time and shared their constructive feedback with me, especially Stuart Beattie, Isabelle Dickerson, Diana Earnshaw, Melanie Faulks, Maxine Hargreaves, Tanya Ces Maneiro, Hemma Mason, Sabine Matharu, Paola Merlassino, Jennifer Read, Myrna Rickards, Marie Shepherd, Stephanie Smith, Amanda Sumner, Janice Townsend and Christopher Weaver.

CUSTOMER TESTIMONIALS

"Vanessa has a wonderful, natural style of writing which is also incredibly insightful and informative. It's as if she is sitting in front of you, speaking specifically to you, which is how I'd love my clients to feel when they see my content. The whole area of 'Marketing' can feel overwhelming for business owners, but Vanessa cuts through this by starting with your business and what makes it special, which is easy to get excited about it. Everything flows from there. It's as if she is able to help us find our creativity even if we don't think of ourselves as creative."

STEPHANIE SMITH
Career Coach, Stephanie Smith Coaching

....

"Like many people, I use Facebook to keep in touch with friends but know I could use it more to promote my business. However, knowing where to start has always been a challenge - until now! In this no-nonsense guide, Vanessa demystifies the subject by breaking it down into bite-sized, daily tasks, which has given me many new ideas for engaging, unique and authentic content. I can't wait to start creating my posts and building a following. Thank you for the inspiration, Vanessa!"

STUART BEATTIE
The Content Builder

"This is just what I needed! I've been managing several Facebook pages for some time, but was struggling to come up with new things to share. This little book has given me a wealth of new ideas for promoting my wellbeing events. It's brilliant."

DIANA EARNSHAW
Business Owner, Your Good Health ~ Naturally

....

"I love the book! There's a huge amount of content, tips and advice to take in - and that's coming from someone who's technically aware, but not always confident in promoting herself."

AMANDA SUMNER
Website Designer

....

"Thank you, lovely sister, for writing this little book just for me! I had been creating and sharing images on my Facebook page daily, and then I paused due to ill health and stopped. Now I know why. This little book has such a beautiful variety of tips and creative suggestions. Now I can't wait to get started on implementing the ideas in this book and offering more value and creating more interaction with my readers."

MAXINE HARGREAVES
Fresh Air Fridays Facilitator

"I really liked the style of Vanessa's book - the format, flow and the genuine support that seems to exude from it! A lovely book and yes, full of inspiration! I started making notes straightaway and the reminders of 'one day at a time' to ease any overwhelm (for me, about marketing tasks and time) was hugely welcome. I also appreciated the regular invitations to reflect upon my journey and efforts throughout the book. Above all, Vanessa reminds us that we are all unique and that's exactly what her guide and exercises tap in to. It's all about who we are and applying that to Facebook for business - and that's inspiring for confidence, as well as action, isn't it?"

MELANIE FAULKS
Work Psychologist & Life Coach,
Agdela Coaching

"This little book packs a punch! It is full of practical, realistic and creative advice. It's the sort of book that is great for busy people who want to learn whilst doing. The style is perfect, very friendly and encouraging. Vanessa's enthusiasm for this subject really comes across and is infectious! The book will be a great help to anyone who is looking to make the most of their Facebook page and, in Vanessa's words, make it fizz!"

MYRNA RICKARDS
Blue Gem Marketing,
Copywriting and Marketing Services

"As an artist I always felt I needed to have a Facebook presence. I already have a very good website, but something was needed to complement it. Facebook terrified me and I avoided it. Then I heard about this course 'Marketing your art with Facebook' and Vanessa was running it. It was an inspirational day, and since then I've read Vanessa's book. It is clear, it flows well, and pushes your creativity. Vanessa gives you all the tools for running a successful business page and you start to love doing it. Brilliant!"

MARIE SHEPHERD
Sculptor

....

"I'm not particularly great with social media. I don't do much personally and therefore struggle with doing it for my business. It's all the usual things; I I don't know what to post, I always think no-one will want to listen to what I say etc.

Having read the 'Facebook Inspiration' book I'm really excited to start implementing the ideas. I love the way there are small bite-sized bits of information for each day, tasks that you follow and build on as you go forward. I can see that by just doing each small task every day, by the end you will have formed a habit of posting and have a clearer idea of what to post. I highly recommend reading it and seeing what it can do for your page."

HEMMA MASON
Architectural Photographer

"Surround yourself with the dreamers and the doers, the believers and thinkers, but most of all, surround yourself with those who see the greatness within you, even when you don't see it yourself."

Edmund Lee

INTRODUCTION

Welcome to thirty days of creativity to boost your confidence and your Facebook page!

I'm delighted you picked up this book. I'm guessing you spotted it because your Facebook page is looking sad and forlorn. Your friends 'like' your page, but you want to increase your followers and make more impact. You would love to inspire lively conversation on your page and create a Facebook community who support your brand.

Let this handy book, packed with ideas and inspiration, become your trusted Facebook friend for the next thirty days and beyond. It will guide you step by step in establishing a lively business page that's rich with useful information.

The inspiration for this book? My valued clients. The small business owners who are doing what they love, but don't quite know how to share their passion in a way that generates more business.

Just to be clear, this book isn't about marketing strategy. It's not really aimed at huge corporates driving massive marketing campaigns (although I'm secretly sure they'll find some useful tips in here too!) It's intended for businesses that don't have a marketing department. It's for small business owners who know that they ought to be doing 'something' on Facebook to market their business, but they're not entirely sure what that something looks like.

Facebook represents a significant marketing opportunity for small local businesses. The number of Daily Active Users reported by Facebook for September 2016 was 1.18 billion. This represents a 17% increase year over year[1]. Facebook isn't just a social network for your private life. Facebook also enables you to promote your business and raise awareness of your brand.

[1] Source: Facebook as 02/11/2016

The tips in this book are relevant to owners of any type of business page. They will also give you ideas you can apply to advertising on Facebook.

There are plenty of books, courses and webinars available on how to set up your Facebook page for business, how to create posts and share photos and videos. I provide training to small business owners who need to learn the practical skills first. However, I've learnt that even those who know *how* to post don't always know *what* to post. Sometimes they repeatedly share the same content because they don't realise they could be doing something different. If you're in that category, you probably want to know what sort of things you should post and of course, what really works. You know your business differs from your competitors', but how can you demonstrate that on Facebook?

I guarantee that all you need is a sprinkling of inspiration, and a handful of motivation. Maybe you worry it's going to take hours to come up with ideas and prepare your posts. My promise is that you'll see results if you can commit to spending as little as thirty minutes a day working through this book. Once you get started though, I'm positive you won't want to stop at thirty minutes!

My goal is to stir your creative juices by prompting you to look at things differently. My guiding questions will help you spot opportunities to share something novel. I encourage you to share your personal perspective on the world, because that can't be replicated. That's what makes you stand out from your competitors. Once you're inspired, you'll see how much fun it is, how easy it is and how imaginative you can be. It may even help you appreciate the small things that make this world such a beautiful one.

Anyone who has attended a training course with me will probably have heard me say, "the devil's in the detail." There's tremendous beauty in the detail too. I want you to notice small things. What moments trigger an observation or memory for you? In small businesses, your eyes are the eyes of your business. By paying attention to everything you experience, you'll develop a refreshing outlook to share with your followers on Facebook. From now on, when you see things that spark a creative thought, you must capture that thought and act on it.

Start your Facebook journey now. Block out thirty minutes in your diary and find somewhere comfortable to sit down with this book and a pen. Scribble your creative ideas beneath my daily inspiring questions and plan your Facebook posts. If you run out of space to write your answers, use the **Notes** section at the back of the book, including a reference to the relevant page number.

This is the first book in a series of many. If you follow my suggestions, you'll increase engagement on your Facebook page for business. Then you'll be ready to do the same on Twitter, Instagram, and Pinterest, plus any other social media platforms yet to evolve.

If you'd like more ideas on how to use Facebook to market your business, visit my blog: **www.vanessahunt.co.uk/blog**

P.S. If you've found this little book useful, motivating or inspiring, please don't keep it to yourself. There are lots of small businesses out there that need a hand. Give the gift of inspiration to a friend or colleague. Present everyone in your team with his or her own personal copy. You'll be amazed at how quickly company creativity starts to overflow. And that can only be good for business!

FACEBOOK PROFILES AND PAGES

When you sign up for a Facebook account for the first time, you create a **Facebook profile**. This is your personal page for connecting with friends and sharing updates about your personal life. You control who sees the posts, photos and videos you share on your Facebook profile.

If you want to share information about your business, you must create a Facebook page for business. This business page is connected to your Facebook profile, but in contrast to your profile, a **Facebook page** is always public. This means anyone can view the updates you share on it, which is exactly what you want for marketing!

Facebook provides additional features under **Pages** to help you manage your business page. For example the **Insights** section displays useful statistics about how followers of your page are responding to the content you're sharing. If you have multiple businesses, you can create a different page for each. This allows you to target your marketing to the right audience.

INSIGHTS

You can access the **Insights** section from the top menu on your Facebook page. I review my **Insights Overview** daily, since it provides summary information about the success of your Facebook page. The **Overview** is split into three sub-sections:

- Page Summary
- Your 5 Most Recent Posts
- Pages to Watch

Page Summary displays graphical information about how many people have viewed or liked your page in the last day, week or month. It also shows how many people your page has reached and how many have engaged with your posts, as well as the number of times videos have been viewed.

Your 5 Most Recent Posts shows the reach and engagement of individual posts. It gives you a clear indication of the type of post your followers interact with most.

Pages to Watch is a feature that allows you to see how your page compares to others. You can keep an eye on competitors' pages, to compare whether you are creating more engagement on your page compared to theirs. You can also review which of their posts have created high engagement, which may inspire you to try out different types of post in future.

"Success is the sum of details."

Harvey S. Firestone

LEARNING TO OBSERVE

This week you'll learn how other businesses use Facebook to market their products and services. Observing what other brands share is a great source of inspiration. The intention is not to emulate them, but to observe what they do that's really working for them.

The reason you admire and are inspired by a brand usually reflects something about your own identity. It's by observing the characteristics of others that you gain a better understanding of your essential qualities.

What should I do?

Take one day at a time. Plan a time slot of thirty minutes to answer the questions and complete the task(s) for each day. The optional 'Expand your ideas' section is intended to trigger more creative ideas. You may choose to complete this right away or in different sitting.

RESEARCH BRANDS YOU ADMIRE

- List three brand names you trust the most:

  1.

  2.

  3.

- Find and like their business pages on Facebook.

- Read the last three posts they each shared on their Facebook page.

- What was the topic of each of their posts?

EXPAND YOUR IDEAS

Are the topics related to a common theme? Even if they're not directly related, is there a loose connection between them? Write a couple of sentences to describe the type of post or articles they share on their Facebook page. Reflect on your own business and note down the topics your customers would expect you to write about.

SPOT WHAT GRABS YOUR ATTENTION

- Return to each brand page you reviewed on day one. Scan each page for a few minutes. Notice whether any posts stand out more than others for you.

- If something grabbed your attention, then like it.

- Write down exactly what it was that attracted your attention to it.

EXPAND YOUR IDEAS

Were there any similarities between the things you liked on each of the pages, even though they're different brands? Did they trigger a memory? Did they make you smile? Jot down a few notes, highlighting key points with boxes, stars and arrows to help show what attracted you most about the various posts.

DEFINE YOUR KEY MESSAGE

- Consider the products and services you offer. How do they help your customers? What themes do they relate to?

- Write down the themes in CAPITAL letters. Would they make sense if you used them as hashtags to describe your business?

Tell me more about...

HASHTAGS

A **hashtag** is a special label used on social media sites like Facebook and Twitter. A hashtag makes it easy for people to find posts relating to a specific theme. You can create and use a hashtag by adding a '#' symbol in front of a word or phrase. The '#' symbol is commonly referred to as a hashtag character. Using the hashtag character with a word or phrase creates a hashtag. You can use a hashtag in the main text of a message or at the end. Searching for that hashtag will return each message that has been tagged with it.

Whenever I share a Facebook tip on Facebook, Twitter, Pinterest or Instagram, one of the hashtags I include is **#FacebookInspiration**. Please start using this hashtag too, so we can bid farewell to forlorn Facebook pages!

- Create four clear messages for potential or existing customers that relate to those common themes. Substitute the words in brackets below with your own words:

I help *(small businesses)* **to** *(find more clients)* **by** *(teaching them to market their business creatively with Facebook)*.

1.

2.

3.

4.

EXPAND YOUR IDEAS

Stuck for ideas? Think about things your customers ask you to help them with. Write down the questions you're often asked. Scribble down your typical answer. Convert that answer into a clear, simple message. Don't forget to add these messages to your **About** section on your Facebook page for business.

LET'S GET CREATIVE AND DOODLE

One way to increase your creativity is to try out new things. Draw a picture that summarises the messages you have just written.

USE VIDEO TO SUPPORT YOUR MESSAGE

- Review the messages you created yesterday. Find an interesting video about one of the topics contained in your message. For example, I might search for "new Facebook features 2017" on YouTube. Watch the video all the way through. Watch it again and make notes on the most useful points.

- What was the most interesting or entertaining point in the video? Could you turn it into a question for your Facebook followers? Here are a couple of phrases you could start with:
  - **What do you think of** (*the new x feature in Facebook*)?
  - **Do you agree that** (*Facebook advertising is worth the investment*)?

- Share the link to the video in a new post. Be sure to include your question and a topic word that starts with a hashtag, such as #FacebookFeatures for my example above.

  #

EXPAND YOUR IDEAS

Check your page to see who liked or commented on the video you shared. Make sure you reply to each comment to confirm you've read them. Reply with further questions to get a short conversation going. How would you describe the individuals who responded to your post?

SHARE INFORMATION IN BITE-SIZED CHUNKS

- How would you summarise the key points in the video in the previous step? Write a list of bullet points that communicate the main ideas.

- What's your opinion of those points? Can you add examples to support your point of view?

- Write a post on your Facebook page that includes your opinion and the summary of bullet points. Ideally, include a colourful image that relates to the topic. Be aware that images are copyright protected, so the best images are ones you've taken yourself. Refer to **Useful Links** on page 109 which lists useful websites of royalty free images for use in your posts.

EXPAND YOUR IDEAS

Write down the number of people who liked what you shared. Did you receive any useful comments that you can acknowledge and elaborate on? Don't be shy about soliciting further details by asking a few more questions.

ELABORATE ON CRUCIAL INFORMATION

- Building on what you shared yesterday, search for another article or blog post that goes into further detail about one of the key points.
- Elaborate on the article, adding new information based on your interest or experience.
- When you share your post, make it more personal by highlighting who the intended audience is. For example: "Something useful for anyone involved in web design..."

Tell me more about...

BLOGS

A blog is an area of a website dedicated to sharing news or regular updates. A blog consists of blog posts, each written on an individual web page.

Each time you add a blog post, the most recent post appears at the top. It's common to categorise your posts, so visitors can easily search the types of post that interest them most. By frequently adding interesting content to your website via a blog, your site is more likely to appear in Google's search results.

Blog posts are often written in a conversational style. They can be informative, educational and entertaining. They're useful because they allow you to incorporate a wider range of content in your website to showcase your work and how your organisation's approach is different to others.

EXPAND YOUR IDEAS

Consider how you could add some unusual information or something visual to make this particular post stand out. Why not edit your post and add to it? Check whether you gain any additional responses.

MAKE YOUR POST MEMORABLE

- Hopefully you've seen some positive response to your first week of posts. Why not try a new angle by adding a music or video clip to the mix? If your theme was #creativity, is there some music you can share that makes you feel more creative?

- Please don't just share the music clip without any explanation. Add a story to it. Say where you heard it last or why it inspires you.

- Did your story generate a few more likes and comments than usual? Did others share their experiences and memories?

EXPAND YOUR IDEAS

Whenever you share content on your Facebook page, your objective is to generate an emotional response. The best way to do this is with beautiful or thrilling visual elements and sound. Let your creativity flow through everything you do. Always think about how you can add a new perspective to each post. Write down what kind of images make you say "That's amazing" or "Wow!"

REVIEW YOUR FIRST WEEK

Hopefully you've begun to identify your target audience and have started interacting with them. You may have already built up a small fan base that's liking and sharing your posts. Are there any special followers who are interacting with you on a regular basis? Don't worry if your followers are a little shy. In week two, you'll learn how to listen carefully to them, in order to get the conversation started.

- What did you enjoy most about the Facebook activities you performed this week?

- What surprised you most about the results and responses?

- What could you do differently next time to ensure your next set of posts is even better?

"I learned no detail was too small. It was all about the details." - Brad Grey

"One of the most sincere forms of respect is actually listening to what another has to say."
Bryant H. McGill

Week 2

LEARNING TO LISTEN

This week you'll learn how to pay attention to the people who like or comment on your posts. In my experience only 20% of people reading your content will actually do or say anything. You'd be surprised at how many people consume your content, but don't disclose it. They may not have time to comment on everything they read or perhaps they just prefer to remain anonymous. Don't be disheartened though. It's rather fun to encourage others to contribute. The way you can do that is by responding to anyone who interacts with your posts. You should demonstrate that you appreciate their input and the fact that they took the time to share their opinion or insights. Always acknowledge your contributors to show that you're listening. Your Facebook page represents your valued business community and they should be treated with care and respect.

Remember...

Take one day at a time. Plan a time slot of thirty minutes to answer the questions and complete the task(s) for each day. The optional 'Expand your ideas' section is intended to trigger more creative ideas. You may choose to complete this right away or in different sitting.

ANTICIPATE QUESTIONS

- Review everything you shared last week. If you had to describe the people who interacted with your page, what characteristics would you use to describe them? Do they have similar interests? Are they in a particular age group? Group similar individuals under an imaginary name. You may find that you attract quite different types.

My imaginary name is:

- Imagine your imaginary person is standing in front of you. What questions might they ask? Do you already have the answers? If not, spend some time searching for helpful articles or resources to share. I enjoy recommending marketing or business books that I've found interesting. Newspaper and magazine articles are also excellent sources of trending information.

- Share a post explaining who you think will find it helpful and why. Don't forget to include a great image and a topic or two to describe it, for example #marketing or #productivity.

EXPAND YOUR IDEAS

Did the individuals you imagined you were writing for respond to your post? Did you get the desired response? What do you think they liked most about your curated content?

ASK PEOPLE WHAT THEY'D FIND HELPFUL

- Explain in your post that you'd like to make sure you're sharing the right kind of information. Include a fun hashtag like #JustCurious or #HelpMeHelpYou.

- Ask your audience what they'd like to read about. Just ask a straightforward question, including an image to attract interest.

- Thank everyone who shares his or her opinion. Tell them how you're going to address their topic and when.

EXPAND YOUR IDEAS

How did this exercise inspire you? Could you write a blog post that includes more than one of the topics your audience is interested in? Sketch a rough structure for your future blog post. Sometimes recording your thoughts on a recording device first, and then listening back to them, can help you get going. Even if you just write ten words a day, your brain will keep working on your blog post subconsciously. Capture those ten words. Gradually they'll add up to hundreds.

FIND TOPICS YOUR FOLLOWERS WILL LOVE

- Look around you right now, wherever you're sitting. Is there anything that catches your attention? Something you think might interest your followers too? For example, I'm gazing at a tin on my table called 'Receipts (for money I used to have)'. I use it to store my business receipts before I process them.

- Take a photo of whatever it is or search online for a representative photo.

- What can you add to the photo to make it more interesting? Can you ask a relevant question or add a quote? I might ask 'What systems do you have in place to keep yourself organised?' Spice it up with some hashtags (#CRM, #productivity). Then share it!

EXPAND YOUR IDEAS

How much interaction did you create? Was it the photo or the quote that you think people liked most? How could you improve your approach next time? Did any of the comments surprise you?

SHARE WHAT YOU'RE LEARNING

- Think about anything you've learnt in the last week, whether it was gleaned from a book or an online course. What was the underlying theme?

- Share one key point you learnt and why it's important. Reference the chapter or module specifically, to prove you really read or watched it!

- Ask a question that encourages the reader to share their perspective on that point or to add new ideas to the list.

EXPAND YOUR IDEAS

Did your followers come up with new books or courses that interest you? Were you surprised at how much information people shared? Why do you think they took the time to respond?

STUDY WHAT YOUR FOLLOWERS ARE SHARING

- Write down the names of the five most engaged people who follow your page.

  1.

  2.

  3.

  4.

  5.

- Review their personal profile or their Facebook business page. Did they recently share a Facebook post? What was the article about? Is the page they shared also a page that could be relevant to you and your business?

- Write down the top five topics that were recently shared by your followers. Do a Google search to find articles with similar tips. Add your opinion about what's likely to be most useful for your readers.

1.

2.

3.

4.

5.

 EXPAND YOUR IDEAS

What do you think prompts people to share? Is it to inform, entertain or inspire? Consider the posts you share. Are the inspirational posts shared more frequently than the informative ones? Find out what your followers love sharing.

REMINISCE!

- Your work memories remind people what you do. Can you find a colourful photo from a recent work exhibition, conference or trip?

- Ask yourself what the photo represents for you. What does it remind you of about your job and the work you do?

- Explain why you love the photo and add a hashtag, such as #LoveMyJob. Ask followers why they love their job and encourage them to share their own photos in the comments.

EXPAND YOUR IDEAS

What do you think made people respond to your photo? Did it remind them of their own experiences? Did they love the fact that you were doing something you loved? Did you inspire them to think positively about aspects of their own work that they love?

BOOST THE PROFILE OF ANOTHER BUSINESS

- Think of a business that really supports you and has similar values to you. Make a note of their Facebook page name.

  Facebook page name:

  Values:

- Find an article you've read recently that you know would be of interest to that business. Perhaps it's linked to what they do or how they do it.

  Article title:

- Share that article (it can be a photo of a paper article or a 'real' electronic one!), ensuring that you use a hashtag to highlight the theme.

  #

EXPAND YOUR IDEAS

Keep a list of businesses that regularly support you. How can you promote them on your business page? Is there a way to celebrate their successes?

WHAT WERE THIS WEEK'S HIGHLIGHTS?

This week you hopefully started to learn what type of posts are of most interest to your audience. Notice that people will sometimes like or share an individual post, but not necessarily like your page right away. There's nothing wrong with that. The fact that someone liked or shared a post still increases the chance of others being notified of it, so post likes are still valuable. If a person regularly likes posts on your page, Facebook recognises this activity and assumes that they wish to continue being notified of your updates. The next step is to try to encourage those who like a post to also comment on it and share it. When you regularly see lots of comments on your page, you know you're sharing the right content for your audience. If you're confident about your content, then it's easier to be true to you and your brand. In week three, you'll learn how to communicate precisely what makes your business different.

- What did you enjoy most about the Facebook activities you performed this week?

- What surprised you most about the results and responses?

- What could you do differently next time to ensure your next set of posts is even better?

"The measure of a conversation is how much mutual recognition there is in it; how much shared there is in it. If you're talking about what's in your own head, or without thought to what people looking and listening will feel, you might as well be in a room talking to yourself." - Dylan Moran

"When you are authentic, you create a certain energy. People want to be around you because you are unique."

Andie MacDowell

Week 3

BEING AUTHENTIC

A company's brand is defined by how individuals perceive it. You can always tell when marketing communications aren't in line with a brand. They make you feel slightly awkward! For small business owners, your personality is your brand. If you behave in a way that doesn't reflect your personality, your customers sense it. You need to feel comfortable with who you are, what you value and how you wish to conduct business. Once you're at ease with your personal brand, marketing yourself and your business is effortless.

Remember...

Take one day at a time. Plan a time slot of thirty minutes to answer the questions and complete the task(s) for each day. The optional 'Expand your ideas' section is intended to trigger more creative ideas. You may choose to complete this right away or in different sitting.

HOW DO PEOPLE DESCRIBE YOU?

- What do your customers value about you and your business? How do they tend to describe you and your products and services? You might find it helpful to refer to customer feedback you've received. I'd summarise this testimonial from CBJ Digital Ltd, a digital marketing agency, with 'good with words':

> *The care, research and interest that Vanessa takes in preparing blogs and social media content for CBJ Digital has been impressive. It is lovely to have found a copywriter and social media expert who* **achieves standards that would grace any corporate website** *- that is to say: standards in copy, standards in grammar, standards in spelling! Excellent - thank you.*

Malcolm Iliff, Director of CBJ Digital Ltd

- Could you use any of your customers' descriptive words as hashtags in your marketing? If they're too specific, can you invent a more general hashtag that broadly covers them all? I use #words because it incorporates multiple themes, including writing copy, grammar and my passion for learning foreign languages. I also use #KeepItSimpleMarketing (sometimes shortened to #KISM).

- Share an article that's clearly described by one of your hashtags. Make sure you include a reference to the hashtag within your post, in order to highlight the value you provide to your customers.

 ## EXPAND YOUR IDEAS

Do you feel excited about your list of hashtags? Do you feel more focused about your business direction? Do you see how using hashtags consistently keeps your marketing messages on Facebook cohesive? On a scale of 0 to 10, colour in below how excited and confident you feel about your list of hashtags. If you're still not sure about how to choose hashtags, or if you rate under 5, you can refer to my blog for further guidance.

0   5   10

WHAT MAKES YOU QUIRKY?

· Is there something you used to do as a child that would surprise people? Perhaps you won an award? Perhaps you lived in an unusual place? Did you volunteer or play a musical instrument? You don't have to always be selling on your Facebook page. It's about building a following of people who like and believe in the authentic you. Selling is based on building relationships and trust, which means letting your followers get to know the real you.

· How are those childhood activities reflected in your life now? I was a bookworm and spent hours in the local library every Saturday. Today, I still love reading and discovering unusual words. I think #words are simply wonderful! Dig deep to recall your childhood passion and reflect on how it has made you who you are today.

· Share a photo of your favourite book or a clip of your favourite activity. Add a sentence about how it has affected what you do today. Revel in remembering how far you've come and how it's showing up in your business.

EXPAND YOUR IDEAS

How do you feel thinking about your childhood memories? Do you feel excited to be rediscovering a part of you that you'd maybe forgotten? Or do you feel proud that you persevered with something that's been an interest for a long time?

HOW DO YOU DO WHAT YOU DO DIFFERENTLY?

- We all have competitors. But how are you different from yours? What experiences have you had in your life to make you approach things differently? Write them down.

- Looking at your experiences, what's the common theme? Are you well travelled? Have you had lots of different jobs? Are you meticulous about details? Are you quick to learn new skills? Are you good at asking pertinent questions when conducting your research into new products or services you should offer?

- List the top three things that make you different. Think about what you've done in the last six months that provides evidence of your different approach. Schedule one Facebook post a week that includes that evidence. You could share a testimonial from a happy customer. Or you could share a blog post that demonstrates your expertise or shares your personal experience.

Tell me more about...

SCHEDULING POSTS

Facebook prefers posts that are scheduled with its own **Publishing Tools**. Scheduling is easy. You write your post, then schedule when you would like it to be shared on your page. You can prepare posts in bulk, in advance, and publish them at regular intervals throughout the week or month. If you change your mind about your scheduled date, you can modify it at any time.

If you'd like to learn more about scheduling, I regularly update my blog to include the latest Facebook tips: www.vanessahunt.co.uk/blog

EXPAND YOUR IDEAS

Were you aware of how your personal experience enables you to provide your product or service differently to your competitors? Do you feel a sense of satisfaction knowing that your business has something unique to offer? If you ever feel deflated in future by what your competitors are doing, come back to your notes in this section and remind yourself of what you do differently - and why.

LET'S GET CREATIVE AND DOODLE

One way to increase your creativity is to try out new things. Draw a picture that summarises the messages you have just written.

WHAT DOES YOUR LOGO SAY ABOUT YOU?

- How can you use your logo to convey a stronger brand image? Is your logo represented by an icon or object that you can reinforce by sharing similar images? Perhaps an illustration that you've seen on a book cover? Consider ways you can incorporate your logo into your clothing and appearance.

- I chose a butterfly for my logo because 'Vanessa' is a type of brush-footed butterfly. For me, butterflies imply boldness and transformation, which are core themes in my marketing services. Does your logo evoke any particular words? Could you incorporate them into your business vocabulary?

- Write a post that includes one or two of the words you just listed. Include some breathtaking images to reflect the meaning of the words.

EXPAND YOUR IDEAS

Keep looking around for ideas that could help you maximise the use of your logo. Look for inspiration from other businesses in an entirely different field. Use all your senses to scrutinise the use of language alongside any company logo.

WHAT COLOURS REPRESENT YOU?

- What colours do you incorporate in your brand? Is there a print or poster style that's similar to your colour palette? Take a look at art websites for inspiration.

- Could you create a collage of images in similar colours that reflect your brand and style? Or could you take photos of your own things that match your brand colour and somehow represent what you do?

- Why not share an inspiring motivational quote with your new colourful collage? And don't forget to include a pertinent hashtag!

EXPAND YOUR IDEAS

Where else could you use your new colourful image creation? Did you learn more about the things you find attractive? Is there a font that speaks to your brand? Make a list of websites where you can find similar material to share.

HOW DO YOU SPEND YOUR FREE TIME?

- What do you do when you're not working? Do you have a favourite sport or social activity?

- What is it about this pastime that you enjoy? Is that something you also experience in your business?

- Is there a way that you could bring elements of your personal hobby into your work? Could you share a photo or an article that might be interesting? Perhaps your hobby helps you relax and inspires you in your work? I relish reading fiction, but I also read a lot of books for business. I share the best ones on the **Resources** page on my website, so my customers can benefit from them too.

EXPAND YOUR IDEAS

On a long-term basis, how could you include more of what you love doing in your free time into your work? If you love walking, could you hold meetings whilst walking? If you love music, can you find ways to listen to your favourite music more often – maybe whilst performing mundane tasks?

WHAT TYPE OF WORK MAKES YOU HAPPY?

- What are the things about your work that bring you the greatest joy? Do you have photos of yourself doing those things?

- Write a post called "A day in the life of a (Marketing Consultant)" and explain the key things you do each day. If you'd like to add an alternative angle, try starting with: "10 unexpected things you didn't know about (CRM Consultants)"

- Explain what it is that you love most about your job and how that benefits your customers.

EXPAND YOUR IDEAS

Running a business means we sometimes have to do tasks we don't like doing. Consider ways that you could reduce the time you spend on tasks you don't particularly like doing, but have to do. Can you outsource? Can you use technology to help you? Can you invest in expertise from others to help you do more of what makes you happy?

Tell me more about...

OUTSOURCING

Outsourcing means buying services from other businesses, to allow yourself more time to focus on your own business. Many small businesses outsource the management of their finances, but are hesitant about outsourcing other activities that would save them time. There are many Virtual Assistants who can provide an extra pair of hands to help you with the administrative aspects of running a business.

WHAT ACTIVITIES COULD YOU OUTSOURCE?

Tell me more about...

TECHNOLOGY

When you run a business, you need systems in place to ensure you manage it effectively. Many small businesses use Customer Relationship Management (CRM) systems to help them do so. Most CRM systems include features to help you find new leads, create marketing campaigns, follow up your communications with potential and existing customers, and of course, provide customer service. It is an investment that will save you time, but also ensure you provide your products and services professionally. I'd be lost without my CRM!

HOW COULD NEW TECHNOLOGY SAVE YOU TIME?

WHAT WERE THIS WEEK'S HIGHLIGHTS?

This week was all about being you. Sometimes small business owners feel embarrassed about promoting themselves and their business. You shouldn't. If you stay quiet, you prevent others from benefiting from the products and services you offer. My guess is that your likes and comments increased this week, because you shared content that demonstrated your personality. I am always amazed at how successful some of my more personal posts are. Your followers relate to you as an individual, so don't be shy about sharing what motivates and inspires you. Sharing your real personality means people relate to the authentic you. In week four, you'll learn how to take another confident step forward and start being more vocal about your views and opinions. By the end of the month you'll be leading the way with your inspiring Facebook posts!

- What did you enjoy most about the Facebook activities you performed this week?

- What surprised you most about the results and responses?

- What could you do differently next time to ensure your next set of posts is even better?

"If you're authentic, people smile because they sense there's a piece of themselves there." - Bonnie Hunt

"It took me quite a long time to develop a voic[e]
and now that I have it, I am not going to be
silent." - Madeleine Albright

Week 4

FINDING YOUR VOICE

It's your final week of creativity for your Facebook page. You're probably feeling more convinced that the content you're sharing is relevant to your audience. I'm sure that you're seeing more likes, loves and sharing on your Facebook page as a result of your daily efforts. This should all increase your confidence and confirm that you're doing the right things. In this final week it's time to make your message even clearer and validate your writing style. Let's finish by honing your writing voice so that it works for you and drives results.

Remember...

Take one day at a time. Plan a time slot of thirty minutes to answer the questions and complete the task(s) for each day. The optional 'Expand your ideas' section is intended to trigger more creative ideas. You may choose to complete this right away or in different sitting.

WHAT'S YOUR TONE OF VOICE?

- In my experience, more personal posts typically achieve a better response than purely factual or news-related posts. How could you make something that is heavily informative even more relevant to your audience on a personal level?

- Do you have an unusual story about a client you helped recently?

- When you share wider news, how could you relate to it at a more local level?

EXPAND YOUR IDEAS

Take a look at your local newspaper or a local magazine. Are any local businesses mentioned who are relevant to your business? Perhaps there's a café that you frequent for business meetings. Think of a way of introducing them into one of your future posts.

WHO INSPIRES YOU?

- Who do you admire and why? Who do you sound like? Is your tone similar to theirs in some way?

- Can you find any quotations by that person that would be relevant for you to share?

- Can you link the quote or phrase to a recent experience you've had. For example, seeing a film at the cinema or reading a book?

EXPAND YOUR IDEAS

Take photographs of films or books you see advertised that relate to your business. Remember to include the name of the bookshop or cinema where appropriate. Schedule your Facebook posts to coincide with the launch of the film or book you recently saw or read.

WHAT ARE YOUR BELIEFS?

- Is there something about the way you view your industry sector that's unusual?

- Where does your belief come from? What experiences have helped you form that belief?

- Share an article that says the opposite to what you believe. Add a couple of sentences explaining your alternative view, and why you think differently.

EXPAND YOUR IDEAS

Write a blog post that develops your opinion further. Be sure to include a variety of sources as input, so that you share a balanced view. Demonstrate your passion for your sector by keeping up-to-date with trending topics.

SHARE YOUR BELIEFS ABOUT THE FUTURE

- How do you think you and your competitors need to adapt in future?

- What is your advice for businesses in your sector?

- What activities are you performing to ensure that your business survives?

EXPAND YOUR IDEAS

Don't be afraid of being vulnerable. That's human. Talk to your peers about the challenges in your field. Share your weaknesses and how you're addressing them. Spend time with a team of people who support you and can provide practical advice. Support one another on Facebook by contributing to their posts.

WHAT'S YOUR FAVOURITE MARKETING?

- Think of a TV commercial that's running currently. Which is your favourite and why?

- Is there any link between the ad and your business? Could you relate them somehow?

- Share a link to the marketing video with a relevant hashtag. Include some introductory text about why you like it and how it relates to your business.

EXPAND YOUR IDEAS

Watch as many short videos as you can about your field. TED Talks and TED-Ed have some wonderful videos to inspire. The more content you consume, video or otherwise, the more ideas you'll come up with.

SHARE A CUSTOMER TESTIMONIAL

- Ask one of your most recent happy customers to write a short testimonial about your business.

- If you sell to businesses, suggest the customer provides a photograph of them or their product or service, which you can post alongside their company name and website address. If you sell to individuals, they may prefer to remain anonymous, so you could use initials or a fictitious name to respect their privacy.

- Write a thank you post to share the testimonial and photo. Highlight what makes your customer such a great client to work for.

EXPAND YOUR IDEAS

Think about customers you've worked with in the past. Make sure you're following their Facebook page, if they are also businesses, so you can interact with them regularly. They may share content that would be valuable to your followers. Remember that sharing posts from other Facebook pages to your own is an excellent way to create collaboration between small business owners.

IDENTIFY YOUR MOST POPULAR POST SO FAR

- Review the last month of posts you've shared. Which post proved most popular?

- Write down two or three possible titles for blog posts, inspired by your most popular post. If you're having problems getting started, try coming up with a short title that suggests a problem that needs solving, such as:
    1. The top five ways to (increase your Facebook followers).
    2. How to increase (your level of engagement on social media).
    3. What (salespeople) don't know about (CRM systems).
    4. Why (websites) must be (responsive).

- Choose the blog post title that gets your creative juices flowing. Write your blog. Review it. Edit your title. Edit your blog. Share your first draft and ask your readers for feedback.

EXPAND YOUR IDEAS

Are you feeling clearer about your business identity? Do you understand why your product or service is different? Are you noticing more opportunities to come up with creative posts to share? Have you started to love posting on your Facebook page? If so, please visit Vanessa Hunt Consulting on Facebook and share your success with me!

IMPROVE ON YOUR LEAST POPULAR POST

- Review the last month of posts you've shared. Which post proved least popular?

- Think about the tips you've learnt. How could you improve it now?

- Share your new version of this post and review the **Insights**.

EXPAND YOUR IDEAS

Analyse what didn't go so well with the first attempt at that post. Consider whether this is something that is common to other posts you've shared. What guidelines can you write down for yourself, so you don't repeat the error in future.

BE RESOURCEFUL TO IMPROVE YOUR WRITING

- The best writers read. Ask five of your closest work colleagues or peers what their favourite marketing blog is.

- Read some articles from these blogs. Which blog do you find most readable?

- Plan thirty minutes a week to read similar blogs. Share a link to the blog and describe why you enjoy it.

EXPAND YOUR IDEAS

A useful way to improve your writing is to summarise other people's writing. This helps you improve your ability to digest the key message of the writing. You can write a short review of a book or blog you read and share your digest on your Facebook page. Alternatively, you can write bullet points to summarise the top two messages from the book or blog.

WHAT WERE THIS WEEK'S HIGHLIGHTS?

I hope the last week of using this book has shown you that marketing can be enjoyable and easy if you are true to yourself and your beliefs. I imagine you're finding it easier to express yourself, so you don't have to spend so much time preparing your posts. Ideas of interesting things to share are probably coming thick and fast. Hold tight - this is only the beginning!

- What did you enjoy most about the Facebook activities you performed this week?

- What surprised you most about the results and responses?

- What could you do differently next time to ensure your next set of posts is even better?

"The one thing that you have that nobody else has is you. Your voice, your mind, your story, your vision. So write and draw and build and play and dance and live as only you can." – Neil Gaiman

"Make it simple, but significant."

Don Draper

WHAT WAS YOUR HIGHLIGHT OF THE MONTH?

Congratulations on posting on Facebook for thirty days! You've developed a wonderful new habit that will help drive business to your website.

Some posts require more preparation than others and you may not feel confident in all areas just yet, but you've tried out lots of new things. Perhaps some posts didn't work the first time, but that's no reason to suggest they wouldn't work another time with a few tweaks. Don't give up - your audience will grow more confident in liking and commenting, as you grow more confident in sharing regularly on Facebook. I trust that you've discovered a creative side to you that you maybe didn't realise you had!

Take five minutes to reflect on what you've learnt and experienced this month. What were your highlights? What type of post was easiest for you to create and share? Where did you feel most comfortable? Which posts surprised you in the volume of response you received to them?

I hope you are feeling motivated to continue.

GOOD LUCK!

"It does not matter how slowly you go, as long as you do not stop."
Confucius

FINAL WORDS

Congratulations on creating thirty compelling posts to market your business on Facebook. I hope you've enjoyed working through this book as much as I enjoyed writing it. You may have been surprised to discover that you have an inner marketing muse after all. Consider this book the beginning of your creative journey!

"It doesn't matter where you start. Only that you begin."
Robin Sharma

Before I started writing 'Facebook Inspiration', I analysed the way I generate ideas for my own page, Vanessa Hunt Consulting. I reviewed the **Insights** for my page to see which posts resulted in the most likes, comments and shares. This book is a summary of my personal experience. I recommend checking your Facebook **Insights** every day to review where you're personally achieving the best results.

Long-lasting relationships must be nurtured. It takes time to create a community who trust you enough to share your content with their friends and followers. I love how Facebook pages enable you to create conversations with your community in ways that other social media platforms don't. By investing just thirty minutes in your page every day, you will gradually see the number of likes increase. You'll gain followers who genuinely like the content you're sharing.

There's no magic number for how many followers a Facebook page should have. However, I've witnessed that high quality followers convert into sales.

By regularly updating your Facebook page, your followers will get to know you, recognise what your brand stands for and gradually trust you. This means you don't have to be pushy. Instead, you can educate and inform potential clients. Personally, I find this a much more satisfying and rewarding way to develop business.

I'd love to see you continue with your new creative habit. Why not grab another copy of 'Facebook Inspiration' right now? It will help you produce your next set of creative posts for your growing Facebook page. Creativity increases the more you use it. You made a great start this month, but I suspect your insights will be different again next month. Let me know how you get on.

Mention **#FacebookInspiration** to share your success with me. I'd love to hear from you.

Wishing you well,

Vanessa
Advocate of keeping marketing simple
#KeepItSimpleMarketing

ABOUT THE AUTHOR

Vanessa Hunt is a quadrilingual marketing consultant and trainer with expertise in communications and technology. Vanessa is the creator of Facebook Inspiration, the first in a series of business books designed to tease out your creativity, so you can market your business more effectively.

This book was born out of practical marketing workshops and conversations with small business owners who were struggling with what to say on Facebook and weren't seeing results from their marketing efforts. Vanessa has blended her marketing experience and love for transferring skills and building confidence in others into this inspiring book.

Vanessa is a keen linguist, fluent in English, French, German and Italian. She's worked on a variety of technology projects, delivering CRM training across Europe in multiple languages. She loves travelling, reading and helping other small business owners create a life they love.

Find out more about Vanessa at:
www.vanessahunt.co.uk

"At some point in life the world's beauty becomes enough."

Toni Morrison

USEFUL LINKS

You've learnt the importance of including powerful images in your posts. Here's a selection of websites where you can find royalty free images. Please ensure you refer to each site's guidelines regarding attribution of images for commercial use.

www.pixabay.com
www.unsplash.com
www.pexels.com
www.morguefile.com
www.freemagebank.com
www.freeimages.red
www.foter.com

Can't find the image you're looking for in this list? Here's a comprehensive blog article from Canva Design School listing the '73 best sites to find awesome free images':
https://designschool.canva.com/blog/free-stock-photos

Feeling adventurous? Want to make your posts stand out? How about incorporating some branding in your images? You can use some fantastic free software called Canva to create simple images with text and your logo. Visit **www.canva.com**. Canva is very easy to use and there are lots of tutorials if you need a little help.

And lastly, if you want to make your posts even more fun, here are some cool symbols you could use on your Facebook page:
www.fsymbols.com/all

"Be truthful, gentle, and fearless."

Gandhi

ACTIONS I NEED TO TAKE

To ensure you benefit further from this book, note down immediate actions you wish to take. For example, are there any blogs you want to read, books you want to buy, websites you want to visit or new skills you need to acquire?

"Wherever you are, be all there."

Jim Elliot

LET'S KEEP THE CONVERSATION GOING

Search **#FacebookInspiration** on Facebook, Twitter, Pinterest and Instagram for new content related to this book.

Keep up-to-date with the latest Facebook news by reading my blog and liking my Facebook page:
www.vanessahunt.co.uk/blog
www.facebook.com/VanessaHuntConsulting

VANESSA HUNT CONSULTING

For creative book design and publishing, visit Chrystel Melhuish's website and like her Facebook page:
www.plumdesignpublishing.com
www.facebook.com/PlumDesignPublishing

Plum Design & Publishing

NOTES

NOTES

NOTES

NOTES

NOTES

CPSIA information can be obtained
at www.ICGtesting.com
Printed in the USA
BVHW020802221019
561747BV00009B/214/P